From Grief to Grace . . .

An Upward

Spiral of Healing

A Guide to Finding the Good

In Unspeakable Sorrow

From Grief to Grace . . . an Upward Spiral of Healing

DEDICATION

I lovingly dedicate this book to
Resh Michael Ortego,
my precious, beautiful youngest son,
and to my two older sons, Troy and John Ortego.
I am so blessed to be your mother
and to learn from each of you the healing
power of unconditional love.

Resh Michael Ortego
April 17, 1977 - July 25, 2013

From Grief to Grace . . . an Upward Spiral of Healing

From Grief to Grace… an Upward Spiral of Healing

A Guide to Finding the Good in Unspeakable Sorrow

Introduction

Welcome…you have found your way to a path full of potential, even though perhaps in this very moment, that potential may not be at all apparent. If you are reading this, I suspect you may have experienced a breaking of your heart—an event in your life which took you deeply into the domain of sorrow—an event that feels like a devastating loss. Whether you purchased this book or it was given to you, you are in the perfect place to begin your healing journey. I believe your soul has led you right here to this moment.

I was both inspired and compelled to write this book. My hope is that it becomes a working document, a sort of journal and captain's log, which helps you, the reader, to chart your course through the turbulent waters of pain and guides you to a safe-harbor on the other side of the storm. By capturing the pain with your pen, it's possible to release its grip on your heart and find your peace. I know, because I've done it. I kept notes as I was deep in my own process, and when I emerged, I could see a pattern to the healing, an upward spiral.

I want to wrap my arms around you and assure you it will all be okay. If you let the grief give you its gifts, you will open a doorway to awareness and a deep connection to yourself—to your strength, your resilience, and your capacity to experience love and joy. I speak from personal experience. The soil of sorrow can be rich with blessings, but only if you use it to grow your spirit. The temptation exists to let it devastate and bury you rather than elevate and open. But not you. You are here, and you found your way to this more empowering way to work with your grief.

The full story of my own journey is told in the book I wrote within the first eleven months after my youngest son Michael's death in July 2013. Called *From Grief to Grace...A Mother's Journey*, it's available through Amazon. Writing that book fulfilled a promise to my son—one I made after his passing. This book fulfills a promise made to myself—that I would share what I learned so others might find comfort, and do it in a format that invites the reader to actively engage, beyond just reading the book. It's an invitation to journal, even if you don't think of yourself as a writer, but more than that, it's an invitation to explore and be curious and meet that part of us that knows our heart and our strength.

I am just one person who found my way and took some good notes so I could map out the territory. I'm sure mine's not the only way. My hope, however, is that by reading this book and doing your own soul searching on the pages provided, you, too, will find the good in unspeakable sorrow. You, too, will step through the grief and find that the spiral of healing has lifted you up into a state of grace and gratitude that may seem impossible and out of reach at the beginning of your journey.

This I do know for sure—wholeness and joy and laughter await you. Feel a big hug from me as you step into your own spiral of healing.

Every day is a Gift

Words to be written or a truth to be lived?
Every day is a gift.
A platitude or truly gratitude realized?
Breath of life, eyes to see, ears to hear,
My hands to touch, and my tongue to taste.
Every atom and cell in my body alive,
Working to keep my unit working
So I can enjoy and participate in life.
I can communicate.
I can listen and I can love.
And, I can go to sleep, unaware, numb to it all,
Busy, busy with circumstances,
Or I can awake to the realization that each moment is precious.
Each day lets me shine my light and be a blessing
Each day I get to choose to see life as a gift
Thank you for this day.

by Robyn DeLong

Finding the Good in Unspeakable Sorrow

"This is good." "How can this be good?" "No, this is good." As you read the short tale that follows, ask yourself, are you more like the king or the servant?

Once upon a time, in a small village in Africa, there lived two close friends who grew up together, sharing many adventures. As it turns out, one of the friends became the king of the village and the other delighted in being his servant and friend.

The servant had a long-standing habit of looking at every situation that ever occurred in his life (positive or negative) and remarking, "This is good!" The king didn't share this attitude.

One day the king and his servant were out on a hunting expedition. One of the duties of serving the king was to load and prepare the guns for the hunt. This day, something went terribly wrong, for when the king fired his gun, it backfired and blew off his thumb.

Examining the situation, the servant did what the servant always did and said, "This is good!" Writhing in pain, the king reacted angrily, "No, this is not good. This is definitely not good!" and ordered his guards to take his friend to the deepest part of the dungeon and leave him there.

About a year later, the king was hunting in an area that he should have known to stay clear of. Cannibals captured him and took him to their village. They tied his hands, stacked some wood, set up a stake and bound him to the stake. As they came near to set fire to the wood, they noticed that the king was missing a thumb. Being a very superstitious tribe, they never ate anyone who was less than whole. So they untied the king and sent him on his way.

As he returned home, he was reminded of the event that had taken his thumb and felt remorse for his treatment of his friend. He went immediately to the dungeon to speak with his friend. "You were right," he said, "it was good that my thumb was blown off." And he proceeded to tell his servant all that had just happened.

"I am very sorry for sending you to this dungeon for so long. It was really bad for me to do this. Please forgive me!"

"No," his friend replied, "This is good!"

"What do you mean, 'This is good'? How could it be good that I sent my friend to prison for a year?"

To which his friend replied, "It's very good! If I had not been in prison, I would have been with you."

I love this story. A version of it can be found in many traditions, sometimes with a king and a rabbi, sometimes a wise hindu monk and a prince. The story is told to teach and inspire trust in a higher good. I've been both the king and the servant at different times, arguing with myself, sometimes so caught in the pain that I don't want to hear anything about how it might be framed as good. We all have both within us. Who will have the last word?

For me, I tend to look for the good or at least try to stay neutral—not labeling something bad or awful. I've learned I get to live with my labels, so I'm mindful of how I speak about people and events. I've been called a Pollyanna more than once and have proudly defended that attitude toward life. Pollyanna-ish has become a derogative term used to put down someone who isn't being realistic. If you read the story of Pollyanna, she was taught by her father to play the "glad game." The goal was to try and find something to be glad about in every circumstance. Her way of being glad transformed a town. Pollyanna is a work of fiction. So is the story about the king and the servant. Yet, they point to a truth that is very real—we are the ones who get to choose what things mean and name them either good or bad. This capacity for choosing gives us dominion over our sorrow if we learn how to use it wisely.

I do my best to look on the bright side when I can remember to do so. I'm not perfect at it, but have made it a high priority because I've learned and experienced the transformative power of tuning in to a higher possibility. And, yes, there are times when the clouds obscure the sun. Sometimes it's not at all apparent that there is something good in whatever happened. Not everyone wants to hear about it either, especially in the middle of the pain. Most of us have heard someone say, "Look for the silver lining." Or, "For every down there's an up." "When life gives you lemons—make lemonade." One of my favorites is, "If the barn is full of horse manure, start digging—there must be a pony in there somewhere."

But what about those times when tragedy strikes, when the pain and sorrow are so intense it makes finding a blessing nearly impossible? There are times when we are plunged into what St. Thomas Aquinas and St. John of the Cross called "the dark night of the soul" where everything we believed about ourselves gets turned upside down. When it feels like we've been cut off from our joy.

I believe that the circumstances of our lives are the curriculum for our spiritual evolution. When do we decide if this is true or not? Is it only true when the curriculum is easy? What about when unbelievable sorrow lands in our lives? When faced with our own dark night of the soul, is it possible to maintain a belief that we live in a friendly, loving universe that is conspiring in our favor, urging us to grow and become all that we can? It didn't feel like a friendly universe when I got the phone call. My practice of looking for the blessing, and knowing I get to choose my response, became my ultimate support and deep source of comfort during my journey out of the darkness.

Thursday, July 25, 2013, began softly, quietly, just an ordinary day. The morning coolness from our Sacramento delta breeze blew gently through my open windows—a beautiful summer day beginning—my morning cup of coffee brewing as I emptied the dishwasher. My youngest son, Michael, age 36, was away visiting his dad. He had called two nights before saying he was going to visit for another night or so. Only the morning sounds of the birds and squirrels and wind chimes filled the air until my phone chirped from my bedroom night stand at 7:35 a.m. That call forever changed my life.

When I answered, my ex-husband's wife identified herself and began telling me what felt like a very long story about Michael and a truck. Maternal alarms fired off inside of me as I asked, "Where's Michael? Is Michael okay?" thinking he must be injured. I heard her say, "I don't want to tell you this."

"Tell me what?"

She repeated herself, "I don't want to tell you this."

And then I heard her say, "Michael's gone."

"Michael's gone? Gone? Gone where?" I asked, wondering if she meant he'd run away which made no sense. My mind could not grasp the impact of the most dreadful words any parent could ever hear.

My knees buckled when the meaning of her words sunk in, calling forth a guttural, wailing, keening sound from the depth of my soul, screaming "No! No! No!" and repeating as every cell in my body shook. I had no place to put this news—no reference or framework to minimize its impact or hold back the tsunami of emotions crashing over me.

I know others have received knee-buckling news. I've witnessed television broadcasts and watched movies where actors vividly portray these tragic moments. Seeing it, even when it's very real, but happening to someone else, never prepared me for the experience of shock, the shaking pain in every cell, the disbelief and denial, the feelings and soul-wrenching sounds of having it happen to me.

No parent could ever prepare themselves for news like this. I certainly didn't see anything good in the death of my precious son. My inner Pollyanna was silenced. I plodded through the next few days, making impossible decisions, preparing to celebrate Michael's sweet life, and dealing with the finality of his death. I wondered if my shattered heart could ever feel whole again. When I looked back at the first five days, from hearing the news to sitting with family and friends on my patio after Michael's celebration of life service, I could see that I experienced the full complement of human feelings and emotions— shock, despair, pain, sadness, numbness, confusion, fear, anger, regret, and a pain in my heart that is difficult to describe. I also experienced hope, as well as laughter, joy, love, compassion, tenderness, gratitude, awe and wonder.

Those emotions continued to cycle through my life for several months as I groped my way through the grief and sorrow. I wrestled with this pain and demanded that it give me a blessing. I held on to the rock of my belief that even in the darkest moments, I could experience hope and love. I turned to Michael, still my best friend even though no longer here in the flesh, asking him for guidance and help. We began learning a new language of connection while I blindly inched my way along the path from pain to peace.

I wasn't sure what possible good could come of Michael's death, but I was determined to see if I could create some. If life dared to take from me such a treasure, then I believed it must absolutely bring me a commensurate positive blessing. This became my quest, my vision—to find the good, to allow it to win with me, to say yes to the sweetness of life, and to light the way for others who find themselves on this path. I refused to become a victim, knowing I could choose my responses if I stayed aware of the choice points in front of me. I have learned a few things first-hand about traversing the gap between grief and grace, ways that I could manage my thinking, and practices I could engage in that moved me forward. This is what I hope you can harvest from working your way through this little book and taking your own notes.

I'm truly able to say, "Yes, my heart has healed." Today, I am stronger yet more vulnerable than ever, and I've captured many blessings along the way. I'm able to refocus my mind, rise above doubts and fears, and think the thoughts that allow me to honor Michael, celebrate the years we had together, and create for myself a new normal that is rich with possibility and promise. I knew I had a choice, and I just kept doing my best to respond in a way that empowered me and helped me feel better, feel more alive, feel more connected. I chose to focus on the beauty and focus on the love and not miss it by being sad and wishing things were different.

"Healing is a progression of mental steps," writes Michael Newton in his book *Destiny of Souls.* I have learned those mental steps can lead us up a spiral of healing if we will accept and surrender to the process. For every journey, there are some helpful tools. For this one, here are five powerful practices that will make all the difference. First, pay attention to your inner world of thoughts and feelings. Next, notice what you are noticing. Third, stay curious and open. Fourth, listen to your heart's wisdom. And, finally, become a conscious chooser. These tools will not only move you up the spiral of healing, but will sharpen your ability to handle any difficult life circumstances you encounter. You will be using these tools throughout the journey.

Acceptance, Surrender, and Immersion

Anyone faced with what seems like an insurmountable wall of grief can experience the spiral of healing. Big impact equals big impact. The impact of what feels like a huge loss—the death of a loved one, especially a child, the ending of a marriage, a prolonged illness—has the potential to either devastate and destroy your life, or transform you, taking you on a journey of the heart that will lead you through a spiritual doorway into a more powerful, connected, and purposeful life. There is an upward flow of healing energy inviting you and pulling you forward into wholeness if you will just step fully into it.

The first turn on the spiral takes you through acceptance, surrender and full immersion into the ocean of sorrow. Acceptance is the doorway into healing—a recognition that you cannot change what occurred. Accepting the reality of what cannot be changed settles down that part of us that wants to fight and struggle against the circumstances and prepares the way for spiritual growth and healing to begin. There is a feeling of peace, surrender, and relief that only occurs when the struggle stops and the breath slows down and deepens—much like when a bird, caught in a snare, settles down for a moment so loving hands can gently cut away the ties that are binding it.

For me, the first turn of my healing spiral was to surrender to the fact that my beloved son Michael was no longer in this physical world. I had to accept the finality of what had happened. No amount of screaming or crying or futile questions about "why?" was ever going to change the reality I was facing. This is the first move—the most basic, fundamental, lowest step onto the spiral of healing—accepting what is so.

At this most elemental level, I learned that numbness is a temporary resting place—not a destination. Shock and numbness and disbelief and a screaming denial of what happened, all must eventually yield to an acceptance of what is. Healing begins with a willingness to step into the depths of our feelings and emotions.

Grief is a very physical experience. Grief hurts inside your body, not just in your emotions. Heartache rips open the walls of your chest with what feels like unbearable pain—an actual, not metaphorical, experience of an aching area in your chest around the heart. It's vital to feel it all fully and to trust that you will survive. The first spiral of acceptance and surrender requires you to fully experience the feelings as they come. It requires the baptism of immersion.

Waves of tears will crash over you, erupting from the chasm in your heart. To avoid immersion, to refuse to surrender to these feelings, does not make them go away. There are those who have tried to skip this part of the journey, thinking they can control an ocean. It's impossible, and the grief will continue to surface until you fully step into it. You can bury a bone but you can't bury a worm. Feelings are just like worms.

Your mind will try to argue against what happened, giving you what-ifs and if-onlys and should-haves and shouldn't-haves. It will search for people to blame. It will want to review and replay and relive all of what happened from every possible angle. These are the snares, the pits, the mental traps that bind you to suffering. Notice them. Write them down in the back of this book. Know as you do this, you will become stronger and these thoughts will become weaker in their ability to entangle you. Begin using your five tools of transformation. As you pay attention, notice and stay curious, you will hear your heart's wisdom and define your choices. When you practice acceptance, you free your energy to begin the journey of healing into grace.

"We are not human beings having a spiritual experience. We are spiritual beings having a human experience." So writes Teilhard de Chardin, (1881-1955), a French philosopher and Jesuit priest who wrote *The Phenomenon of Man*. He also said, "In the final analysis, the questions of why bad things happen to good people transmutes itself into some very different questions, no longer asking why something happened, but asking how we will respond, what we intend to do now that it happened." Both of these quotes point to a perception that needs to be established at the beginning. Who are we? Do we believe there is more to life than what we can perceive with our five senses? Are we merely advanced animals, mortals whose essence ends with our death? If we accept the premise that we are spiritual beings having a human experience, another important distinction becomes: What part of us is doing the choosing?

Let me introduce you to my miniature schnauzer, Chewie. He is about seven, weighs in at 18 pounds, and if he's not groomed, looks very much like a stuffed bear. We are not sure exactly how old he is, or much about his history, as he is a rescue who found his way into my heart just before Christmas 2011. Whenever I go into the kitchen, open a drawer, rustle a package, make any kind of indication that food might be happening, Chewie will come sliding into the room fully alert and hoping for a handout. The speed of his arrival is something to behold. No matter how sound asleep he appears to be, how completely relaxed and off in his own world he looks, he has no choice at the opening of a drawer but to jump up and scurry. He doesn't receive a treat every time. In fact, most of the time he just gets to sniff around the baseboards hoping for a crumb.

We laugh at a dog who jumps at the crackle of a package opening, but where are we doing the same thing? Where are we failing to notice that we have choices about how we'll respond, what thoughts we will pay attention to? Being able to consciously choose requires being aware that a choice is available to us. There is a certain awakeness to our inner world that is called for. The more we can keep our hearts open and stay present, even in the depth of the pain and sorrow, the more we can use our grief to open new avenues of awareness and possibility.

Someone who knew and powerfully demonstrated his freedom to choose his responses is Austrian psychiatrist, Viktor Frankl, author of *Man's Search for Meaning."* Frankl lived to be 92 years of age, from 1905 to 1997, and survived almost four years in multiple Nazi concentration camps including Auschwitz. After his release in 1945, he founded the school of logotherapy and his work has been called perhaps the most significant thinking since Freud and Adler.

Even in the worst imaginable inhumane circumstances, Frankl held firm to the belief that man's spirit can rise above his surroundings. He writes, "When we are no longer able to change a situation, we are challenged to change ourselves. Often it is just such an exceptionally difficult external situation which gives man the opportunity to grow spiritually." Any event which breaks open our hearts with the sword of sorrow brings us face to face with the challenge to change and grow spiritually, to make sense of it all, and to demand a blessing.

Frankl theorized that it was by connecting to a sense of purpose that Holocaust survivors were able to make it through such a trying time. When Frankl was being processed by the SS into the first camp, he stood naked in front of his captors, stripped of his name, his identity, his clothing, even his body hair was shaved off. He was separated from his beloved wife and his parents. He never saw them again, as not one of them survived. The guards destroyed the only manuscript he had of his life's work and made him remove his thin gold wedding band. Nothing was left. Yet, Frankl realized that no one could force him to give up hope, or to hate, or to let go of the possibility that he would survive and be able to continue his work as a psychiatrist.

He writes, "The experiences of camp life show that man does have a choice of action. We who lived in concentration camps can remember the men who walked through the huts comforting others, giving away their last piece of bread. They may have been few in number, but they offer sufficient proof that everything can be taken from a man but one thing—the last of the human freedoms—to choose one's attitude in any given set of circumstances, to choose one's own way. Life is never made unbearable by circumstances, but only by lack of meaning and purpose."

How do we establish the meaning and purpose of something we never asked for? How do we stay open and awake to our choices? With the news of Michael's death, my heart felt like a meteor had exploded into it, creating a crater as deep and massive as the love being ripped from my arms. At the same time that I was experiencing this unspeakable pain, I also became aware of loving waters pouring into me with their promise of healing. I intuitively knew that closing my heart to the pain would also shut down the joy.

The willingness to fully immerse yourself in the experience, to feel the unbearable pain, ultimately allows you to feel the sweet balance of joy which, if you pay attention, shows up as love pouring in from all directions. Teilhard speaks to this. He says, "Joy is the infallible sign of the presence of God." Joy will be there if you welcome and allow it, if you can stay open to the possibility of healing. Sometimes it's impossible to tell the difference between tears of sadness and tears of joy, as they both pour forth from a heart broken open. Let the tears flow.

As you are allowing the feelings to wash over and through you, notice and listen and pay attention to the nuances. You will see that there are beginnings and endings, highs and lows, deeps and shallows, intenseness and softness. This practice of tuning in allows you to connect to your inner knowing, to begin developing that part of you that can notice the pain, feel its raw edges and the depth of the hurt, and be fully with it, fully in it, yet not overcome by it. I call this practice developing a relationship with your inner wisdom or witness. Surrendering into this experience allows you to float to the surface of the pain, to trust the love that sustains and heals and holds you.

I'm using water metaphors. I love and respect the power of water and the images that came to me when I surrendered myself to my own waves of grief. Water and emotions; water and the deep subconscious; water and birth; water and waves; water and lakes, and water filling the scarred and ragged places. Healing waters, soothing waters, and waters that will pull you under if you fight and struggle with them. Eleanor Roosevelt is credited with saying, "All the water in the world can't drown you unless it gets inside of you." Immersion into grief is experiencing it fully, and moving through it and learning to ride its waves so you do not drown.

Since it was the death of my son that plunged me into darkness, I quickly discovered that one way to touch the hem of hope was to cultivate and nurture the belief that it is possible to stay in communication with someone who has passed. You can also learn to listen deeply and watch for the signs and signals loved ones are sending us to say "hello." I have learned so vividly that Michael is just in another dimension, another vibration, and he's very, very present and just as playful and creative as ever. People connect to their loved ones in many, many ways.

Stay curious and engaged and expectant. Pay attention to signs and synchronicities. Learn to recognize the new lines of communication that are being created. Follow the voices of hope and healing. They are out there. Science is beginning to recognize that consciousness cannot be contained in the physical body and isn't destroyed when the container dies. The bonds of love cannot be broken by death.

I have created a new normal that very much includes daily tuning into my son, even if it's just a sweet "hello" and "I love you." Often I feel his presence in my heart space. Tears still flow, but they are now mostly tears of joy and gratitude for our ongoing connection. I find that journaling and quiet time keep me connected to my inner wisdom and to my son. It is vital that you carve out some solitude for your soul.

I continue to learn about and study all of the possible channels of communication with those who have passed from our sight. I have read many scientific double and triple blind experiments, as well as anecdotal stories. (See appendix for a list of titles.) We can commit to learning how to increase our ability to recognize signs and to speak with our loved ones in whatever ways we can, and in whatever language they are teaching us. When we take this on, it helps us to move on into new ways of being with our loved ones and eases the pain of losing the most familiar channel, that of their physical presence here on Earth.

My desire to connect and communicate with Michael grew stronger with each new day, starting from the moment I heard the news and felt him trying to comfort me. Within the first three months, I had read 46 books on the subject of the afterlife, and my research continues. One resource I discovered was AfterLifeTV.com, a site created by private investigator Bob Olson. He began exploring the subject when his father passed in 1998. Olson has collected information and interviewed some of the top researchers and experts in the field, as well as people who have experienced the death of a loved one.

A definitive interview on the subject of afterlife communication is one that Olson did with David Kane. In 2003, a fire erupted in a Rhode Island nightclub, called The Station, claiming 100 lives. The youngest victim was an 18-year-old actor, writer, and musician named Nicholas O'Neill, known as Nicky. Following Nicky's tragic passing, a string of messages, signs and signals from the other side began flowing into the lives of those who loved and survived him. Subsequently, a documentary and book have been made to tell his story.

Olson says this interview with Nicky's father, Dave Kane, is a discussion of those miracles that brought hope and light into the hearts of the grieving. He presents his interview for two reasons: One, for those who have lost loved ones but have not yet recognized any signs from spirit, and two, for those who share extraordinary stories like these where hearing another's story can help you to feel the confirmation that such signs of the afterlife are real. We need each other's stories of hope.

Michael Newton, another student of the afterlife, states, in *Destiny of Souls:* "Survivors must learn to function again without the physical presence of the person they loved by trusting the departed soul is still with them. Acceptance of loss comes one day at a time. Healing is a progression of mental steps that begins with having faith you are not truly alone."

Use the pages in the back of this guide to capture your emotions, your pain, your joy, and the hills and valleys of your journey. It doesn't matter what broke your heart open—death, loss, a diagnosis—take comfort in the Psalmist's encouragement, "Yea, though I walk through the valley of the shadow of death, I will fear no evil, for thou art with me." Notice that the imagery is of walking—not pitching a tent. Be willing to walk and notice and listen to the guidance of your heart. Stare the pain down with your pen, so it moves through your system and out. Write down your observations while they are fresh. This is the beginning of the upward healing spiral.

Trust that the darkness of immersion is rich with learning and will grow lighter as you move forward. You are in the cocoon of awakening. Take good notes. Remain curious. Stay open. Use your tools.

Cocooned

Seems like being cocooned
Is a wonderful way to heal.
Safe from prying eyes,
Tucked in, protected.
Sometimes I wonder.
The caterpillar dissolves inside the cocoon.
Melts into a gooey mess.
New cells start following a new blueprint—
A complete tear-down, not a remodel.
No posts and beams left standing.
A blank canvas,
A miracle.
And—when the butterfly must fly,
The cocoon must go.
And the wings are only strengthened
By pushing through the cocoon.
Working and resting and sensing a new freedom.
Breaking into the light
And flying free.
A wonderful way to heal.

by Robyn DeLong

Emergence, Mindfulness, and Forgiveness

Just as a caterpillar completely surrenders to the chrysalis before emerging as the butterfly, there comes a time for you to complete the work in the cocoon and leave it behind. Give yourself as long as you need. There is no right way to grieve and no timetable to adhere to. Life marches on and you get to choose the cadence that you can handle. There is great value in paying attention to your own unfolding process and mining it for the gold.

The day will come when something inside of you begins waking up to a new way of being—a new normal. Perhaps a day ends and you notice this particular day didn't include any tears. It's the first time. Perhaps something that once triggered you into an episode of sadness passes quietly by, and you feel more peace than pain, more joy than sorrow. This is a time to celebrate. If you've been using the tools of paying attention, noticing, and choosing your responses, you'll recognize this as a positive sign. This is good.

It is also a time to remain alert. For me, my first no-tears day came hand-in-hand with a scary thought that I might be losing my connection to my son. I noticed a fear that my healing would somehow produce a separation and a forgetting, and that in order to hold onto my son, I needed to hold onto the pain. Since I had made it a practice to notice what I'm noticing, I thankfully caught this fear thought and nipped it before it could worm its way into my mind and take root.

I saw this first no-tears day as an indication that my journey had some new places for me to discover. You can also discover more about yourself as you practice being mindful. Notice if your pain is trying to hold onto you. For me, I turned my attention away from the fear and reminded myself of the many ways Michael has of letting me know he's still with me. I treasure these evidences of the continued deep love connection we share even though he's no longer physically present. These are my touchstones for when fear shows up. Begin to develop your own channels of joy.

One very memorable communication happened October 27, 2013, three months after his death, as I was driving. I heard him tell me, "Use joy and laughter to open the channels of communication with the angelic realm. It is the surest channel. Gratitude and joy carry the same vibration." He spoke about a line I love in a song which he wrote "When Angels Whisper." That line is, "I'll meet you at the end of the rainbow, I promise you this. Anytime the rain comes storming, I'm there you can't miss."

I had interpreted this to be a future promise for when I die and pass into his dimension. Michael corrected me. He said, "That promise is for now and the future and always. The rainbow—joy, hope, light in all of its dimensions, primary colors, rain clouds storming—is a bridge of light to follow, and I am always there to meet you—in this present time. I promise. Take my hand. I am guiding you now." These were powerful words for me to hear and left me in a state of awe and bliss. I pulled to the side of the road so I could capture what I had just been told.

As you emerge from your protective cocoon, you, too, will begin to notice that the higher vibrations of love and joy and appreciation are the best wavelengths for connecting to your heart's wisdom. And, if you're grieving a death, this is the best vibration to connect with your loved one's spirit.

Steve Jobs, former CEO of Apple, when faced with his own death, spoke these words, "Almost everything—all external expectations, all pride, all fear of embarrassment or failure—these things just fall away in the face of death, leaving only what is truly important."

With this discovery comes a sweet awareness and mindfulness of each present moment. Your appreciation for life, for the fragileness and preciousness of now, will expand. Knowing at any moment it could all change, could disappear—makes it even more important to pay attention, to express your love, to drink life in.

When you have emerged from the depth of the pain, welcomed joy back into your life, and are standing in the presence of life's gifts right here and right now, you'll become very aware of any thoughts that try to pull you back into suffering. The ability to pay attention to the thoughts you are thinking is vital to this part of the journey. Stay present. Use your tools—notice, listen, choose.

Pain and suffering are different emotional states. Pain is very much in the moment—it comes and it passes. When we fully feel the pain, we can ride its wave from beginning to end. Women who have been through labor pains can easily relate to the rhythm of a contraction. The pain of loss also comes in waves, unexpected, strong, and full of tears—a deep sadness for what is no more. And, it comes to pass—if we let it move through.

Suffering results from holding onto the pain, revisiting the details of what happened, and re-living it over and over. It come from entertaining such thoughts as "Why me? This isn't fair. I can't stand it. I can't take this. This is horrible." It comes from engaging in these conversations with others and building your storyline around it. This is when having a new and empowering story to turn your attention to becomes critical.

A beautiful example of someone who turned a tragic story into an empowering one is Scarlett Lewis. Scarlett is the mother of six-year-old Jesse Lewis who was killed in his first grade classroom during the tragedy at Sandy Hook Elementary School on December 14, 2012, along with 19 of his classmates, as well as six teachers and administrators—one of the worst school shootings in US history. Following Jesse's death, Scarlett wrote *Nurturing Healing Love*, a story about her journey of turning personal tragedy into something that can positively impact the world.

She learned that love was indeed the essential element necessary to move forward, and that taking the path of love is a choice. Scarlett says we can live in anger and resentment, or we can choose love and forgiveness. This grieving mother learned how to choose thoughts of love instead of anger, hatred, or fear, and only a short time after the shooting, Scarlett was able to forgive her son's killer. Scarlett found some peace in spite of this horrifying tragedy and began to believe that choosing love was the key to creating a healthy, safe, and happy world. She began the Jesse Lewis Choose Love Foundation to develop programs to teach children about the power each of us has to change our thoughts and choose a life without fear and hate. Her example teaches us how to shed the burden of anger and hatred in order to find joy again following any tragedy.

You, too, can tell your story so that it has meaning and hope. It is vitally important to find a way to frame what happened so that you are not feeling like the victim in the story. Instead, you are the chooser, the hero, the one determined to find your way through and gather your blessings along the journey. You want to not only guard against the negative, but also have joyful images ready that shift your energy upward.

For me, one of the early images that triggered my pain was that of Michael being struck by a truck and then a car. Gratefully, Michael himself gave me another image within the first 24 hours of the accident. I vividly saw him unfurling his wings and leaping into the light, experiencing none of the pain of the collision. I know he was welcomed by his angels into the everlasting arms of love. I could see these images. Slowly but surely I developed my mental capacity to choose which thoughts I would pay attention to and which images I would focus on. I was training myself in the practice of mindfulness. This is an important rung on the spiral of healing. Whatever images bring you pain, see if you can substitute ones that feel healing to you. Your mind needs an alternative to turn to when the painful images arise, or it will just keep reliving the painful ones.

Sometimes the trigger is anger or blame or guilt. Moving up the spiral requires the practice of forgiveness. Suffering is often linked to our need to forgive—either ourselves or someone else. Helpful questions to journal about are: Who are we blaming? Who didn't do what we would have done? Who is the target of our anger and upset? Listen to your answers. Start with being willing to be willing to be willing to possibly forgive.

Eventually, you will want to forgive everyone, everything. No holding back. It is not for the other person that we practice forgiveness. It's a mental, emotional, and spiritual practice that shifts our perceptions and gives us back our freedom. We do it for ourselves. Forgiveness removes any blocks to our awareness of love's presence and keeps us in the sweetness of life's flow.

Forgiveness is like cleaning your house—you can let it build up for a massive cleanse, or you can stay on top of it bit by bit. Perhaps this is why Jesus answered his disciple's question regarding how many times to forgive with the response, "Seventy times seven." In other words, until the job is complete.

One way to notice if you still have forgiveness work to do is to pay attention to whether someone is safe to walk the streets of your mind. If you want to attack them whenever thoughts of them show up, then you still have forgiveness work to do with them. And, it doesn't matter if they are still living or have moved on. Send them a blessing, knowing it's going to circle its way back to you. Use the back pages of this book to journal your way to freedom.

Notice especially if the target of your attack is yourself. Are you safe in your own mind? One of the people most often in need of a little kindness and forgiveness is oneself. We need forgiveness for not being perfect or super-human, for setting those "always" and "never" impossible standards, for judging others, for not getting everything done, for not being enough, or doing enough, for all of the shortcomings we pile upon ourselves. We need forgiveness, especially if we are carrying blame and guilt, thinking we could have done something to prevent the event causing the pain.

There is a daily practice, sometimes called "doing metta," which focuses on the intention of blessing and forgiving. Practitioners of this loving kindness meditation report that it opens the heart and creates deep feelings of peacefulness and harmony. It is a simple blessing that begins with: "May you be peaceful. May you be happy. May you be well. May you be safe. May you be free from suffering." Then you continue substituting "I" in each sentence beginning with "May I be peaceful. May I be happy...well...safe...free from suffering." And finally, you expand your blessing to include all beings: "May all beings be peaceful. May all beings be happy...well...safe...free from suffering." Repeat this mantra in meditation until you feel the deep peace of it flowing through you.

Use the power of your pen once more to write it all out and release any negative energy still holding you hostage. Remember, forgiveness is always about your freedom, and is not for anyone other than yourself.

I Will Be Blessed

I will be blessed.
I will wrestle with the angels until my gift appears.
I will climb from the well of grief, not drowning,
And command it to teach me.
I will turn from the horror and
Seek the light shining through the cracks of my broken heart.
I will be blessed.
I will learn and grow and teach and heal and
Find my way to be the blessing.
Not someday.
Now.
I am blessed.

by Robyn DeLong

Transcendence, Gratitude and Grace

As you remove the blocks to your awareness of love's presence by doing your forgiveness work, you will begin experiencing a deep sense of peace and oneness with all that is. It's a natural flow through you from the loving life that is breathing you. As Teilhard says, "We are spiritual beings, having a human experience." This next turn on the spiral of healing leads you to transcendence, gratitude, and grace. You now have become a comforter for others who are making their journey through the valley from grief to grace. You have risen above the pain, learned to let go of the suffering and resentment, and have a good start on your forgiveness work. There is a knowing, deep in your soul, that all is well. This state of gratitude and grace fills us with wonder and appreciation for the gift of life and the mystery of creation.

This new normal is full of beautiful new possibilities. Because you have been using your tools of noticing and conscious choosing, you will catch the ways in which old thinking could pull you down. You may have people tell you, "Your heart will never heal. You will always have a hole." You now know this does not have to be the case. It's only true if you accept the thought. You get to choose which thoughts you want to spend time with. Your choice determines if you'll become bitter or better. When you employ your tools of transformation, paying attention, noticing and staying curious, listening to your heart's wisdom, you have the power to choose a higher possibility.

Grief can be your greatest teacher if you stay open and curious and willing to grow through the process. You can arrive at a place of freedom and serenity—a state of grace. It becomes a gift we give to each other as we model what's possible. You can find new meaning and purpose and tell a story of hope to others who need you to shine your light so they can see their way through the darkness. We need each other.

We are called to shine God's light wherever it's needed for those dwelling in the dark places of life – the darkness of one's circumstance, the darkness of a situation a person may have no control over, the darkness of people's limiting beliefs.

In his book *God Has a Dream*, retired Anglican Archbishop Desmond Tutu writes, "If we are to be true partners with God, we must learn to see with the eyes of the heart (and not just the head)....The eyes of the heart are not concerned with appearances but with essences." Tutu goes on to say, "Our suffering can become a spirituality of transformation when we understand that we all have a role in God's transfiguration of the world."

The writer Robert Fulghum tells a wonderful story in his book *It Was On Fire When I Laid Down On It.* He tells his readers about the summer he was a student in Greece, studying Greek language and culture with Dr. Alexander Papaderos who had founded a peace institute dedicated to healing the wounds of war on the island of Crete. At the end of a two-week conference, Dr. Papaderos asked the class, "Are there any questions?"

Fulghum says he responded, half-jokingly, with "What is the meaning of life?"—a question he used to pose as a joke when he was a college student.

"The usual laughter followed," Fulghum said, "and people started to get up and leave." But Dr. Papaderos held up his hand and stilled the room and looked at Fulghum for a long time asking with his eyes if he was serious and seeing from his eyes that he was.

"I will answer your question," he said. Dr. Papaderos then took his wallet out of his hip pocket, fished into it and brought out a very small, round mirror, about the size of a quarter. He said, "When I was a small child, during the war, we were very poor and we lived in a remote village. One day, on the road, I found several broken pieces of a mirror from a wrecked German motorcycle. I tried to find all the pieces and put them together, but it was not possible, so I kept only the largest piece. This one. And by scratching it on a stone, I made it round. I began to play with it as a toy and became fascinated by the fact that I could reflect light into dark places where the sun would not shine – in deep holes and crevices and dark closets. It became a game for me to get light into the most inaccessible places I could find.

"I kept the little mirror, and as I went about my growing up, I would take it out in idle moments and continue the challenge of the game. As I became a man, I grew to understand that this was not just a child's game but a metaphor for what I might do with my life. I came to understand that I am not the light or the source of the light. But light—truth, understanding, knowledge—is there, and it will only shine in many dark places if I reflect it. I am a fragment of a mirror whose whole design and shape I do not know. Nevertheless, with what I have, I can reflect light into the dark places of this world—into the black places in the hearts of men—and change some things in some people. Perhaps others may see and do likewise. This is what I am about. This is the meaning of my life."

And then Dr. Papaderos took his small mirror, and, holding it carefully, caught the bright rays of daylight streaming through the window and reflected them onto Robert Fulghum's face and onto his hands folded on the desk. Fulghum says much of what he experienced that summer is gone from his memory, but in the wallet of his mind he still carries a small round mirror.

The life that Alexander Papederos spoke about is the life we can choose— reflecting God's light in the dark places and spaces in our world, reflecting the light onto the deepest sorrows. We are reminded that our life on Earth is not forever. That time is fleeting. So for the time that we are alive, let's use our time wisely, intentionally, purposefully.

We are the ones who are essential to reflecting the light and shining it into the dark places of grief. I feel like I am following the lead of Frankl, Teilhard, Papaderos, and my own sweet son Michael. He chose to pursue his passion for music and entertaining. His smile would light up the room with his cheerful energy, and he made a difference wherever he went. His life lives on in his music and in all of the hearts of those who love him, especially in my heart—the heart of his mother.

Those of us who have experienced the death of a loved one know first-hand the impact it has upon our hearts. Whatever caused your heart to break, the journey from grief to grace can take you through a doorway into an expanded awareness, a deeper connection to yourself, and your loved ones both here and on the other side. The rich soil of grief can bless us with spiritual gifts we could never have imagined, but only if we are committed and open to looking for them.

We have to be willing to surrender and immerse ourselves fully into the baptismal waters of pain so we can emerge into the light of a new way of being. We must forgive so as to remove our blocks to love's presence. As we use our tools of transformation and mindfulness, we are pulled right up the spiral of healing.

Life is always presenting us with choices for how we will respond. When life gives you lemons, you'd better have some sugar and water on hand if you intend to make lemonade. Sugar shows up as gratitude, possibility, sweet appreciation, a sense of humor, and an ability to create an empowering story out of whatever circumstances have washed up on your shore. Water represents love, strength, resilience, flexibility, and persistence. A drip, drip, drip can carve a canyon over time, and will also work its way into the nooks and crannies of any closed heart.

In the pages that follow, I have given some sentence stems to start with. Feel free to use them or ignore them. You get to choose. The most important action is that you begin to write your way through the grief. Patterns will emerge. Common themes and disempowering beliefs will show themselves so you can challenge them and choose how you want your story to go. Hidden gifts will unwrap themselves as you keep moving forward and demand your blessing.

I have also placed quotes at the bottom of each page. I lovingly chose each of these to inspire and encourage you along the way.

You are in the process of rebuilding your shattered dreams. As you fill these pages, you can look back and see your progress, as well as look forward to what you are consciously choosing, Ask yourself frequently, "What would I love?" "What would it look like exactly?" I know for me, I had to dig beneath my first answer which was, "I would love my son back, whole and safe and as beautiful as ever. I would love for his death to be only a bad dream."

You may be feeling the same way. Just start with the initial step onto the spiral of healing: acceptance and surrender to what happened. Eventually you will begin dreaming up what is next and finding meaning and hope along the way. I know you can do it. You can trust the upward spiral of healing. Life is always calling us forward into a freer, fuller, expanded expression of who we came here to be. Let your grief be the ground from which you grow and nurture your soul.

My hope is that you will use this book as a guide, fill it with your own stories, and use your experience as a doorway into a new, more powerful way of saying "yes" to life. Your story matters. Your light makes a difference. You can fill your life up full with joy and laughter, and you can find your own blessings in unspeakable sorrow.

The world needs our light—yours and mine.

The Power of Focus

I get to choose
My life and my thoughts and my actions.
No one can think my thoughts but me.
I get to choose my focus
And my focus expands and intensifies my experience.
I get to choose.
No one can choose my focus but me.
I choose love and I choose gratitude
And I choose deep listening to my soul and to your soul
And to my loved ones here in flesh and here in spirit.
I get to choose.
It's my life and my gift from my creator.
I get to choose the power of my focus
And the direction it takes me.
No one can choose my actions but me.
I get to choose.

by Robyn DeLong

25 Guides for the Journey from Grief to Grace

1. Feel what you are feeling—fully. Open your heart to all of it.

2. It's okay to cry and it's okay to laugh—all at the same time.

3. Joy and pain balance each other perfectly, if you are open to see and feel it.

4. Numbness is a safe resting place—not a destination.

5. Stay in your heart space, listen to its wisdom, and let it guide all of your decisions.

6. Sleep when you can. Time loses its grip and calendars are of little interest in the early turns on the spiral.

7. Life marches on—you get to choose the cadence that you can handle.

8. Hugging and being hugged are essential to your healing.

9. Say "yes" to helping hands. Let them feed, cook, clean, sort, and hug.

10. Give yourself as long as you need in each turn of the spiral. Listen to your heart.

11. The only right way to grieve is the one that feels most right to you.

12. Notice what you are noticing. Pay attention to your inner thoughts and dialogues

13. Choose which thoughts you want to spend time with. Healing thoughts lift your spirit.

14. Revisiting the pain only brings on more of it. Create empowering images that you can turn to.

15. Regrets, blaming, anger, shoulda's, coulda's, what if's, wish Ida's are all signs for dead-end roads filled with land mines—do not enter.

16. If you notice yourself already on one of those roads, turn around immediately and grab a happy memory to hold on to and pull yourself back.

17. The salt of your tears mixes beautifully with the sweetness of laughter—savor each moment.

18. Some words carry more comfort than others.

19. Forgive everyone everything, including yourself.

20. If you are grieving a death, use your intuition to sense and feel your loved one's presence. Avoid using the term "loss."

21. Watch for signs of hope and healing. Make note of anything that lifts your spirit. You will create more upward movement by doing so.

22. When you speak of what's happening—now, in the future, or in the past—make sure you are the hero in your story and not the victim.

23. Keep a daily journal and fill it with joy and gratitude.

24. Focus on the beauty all around you, don't miss it being sad and wishing things were different.

25. Life is precious. Treat every day as a gift and fill it with joy and laughter and gratitude.

<u>Turns on the Upward Spiral of Healing</u>

Acceptance, Surrender, and Immersion

Emergence, Mindfulness, and Forgiveness

Transcendence, Gratitude and Grace

<u>Five Powerful Life Mastery Tools</u>

1. Pay attention to your inner world of thoughts and feelings.

2. Notice what you are noticing.

3. Stay curious and open.

4. Listen to your heart's wisdom.

5. Become a conscious chooser.

<u>Standing in Gratitude</u>

"Gratitude unlocks the fullness of life. It turns what we have into enough and more. It turns denial into acceptance, chaos to order, confusion to clarity. It can turn a meal into a feast, a house into a home, a stranger into a friend."

Melody Beattie

"We can only be said to be alive in those moments when our hearts are conscious of our treasures."

Thornton Wilder

"If the only prayer you said in your life was 'Thank you,' that would suffice.

Meister Eckhart

"Be thankful for what you have and you'll end up having more. If you concentrate on what you don't have, you never, ever have enough.

Oprah Winfrey

The Healing Power of Journaling

I've been journaling consistently since 1983 when my ex-husband and I separated for the first of three times before finally divorcing in 1994. My sister, Alorah Christina, encouraged me to use my journal as a way of processing what was coming up for me, and also use it as a way of creating what I'd like to experience. I began with a spiral notebook, nothing fancy, and pretty much kept doing just that for the next 30+ years. My only rule for myself was that I date my entries. Decades have passed since those first journals were filled. Someday, I'll go back and revisit some of them. They are safely stored in boxes in my closet and garage. Just the process of taking the time to look within is helpful, even if you never go back and read what you wrote.

I know personally the power of journaling, but for the purposes of this guide, I thought I'd see what some of the research says about journaling. I found only positive encouragement for the practice. Below is an excerpt from an article published online at the University of Rochester Medical Center's Health Encylopedia website:

> When you were a teenager, you might have kept a diary hidden beneath your mattress. It became your confidant and a place to confess your struggles and fears without judgment or punishment. It probably felt good to get all of those thoughts and emotions out of your head and down on paper. The world seemed clearer.

Although you may have ditched the diary once you reached adulthood, the concept and its benefits still apply. Now it's called journaling. It's simply writing down your thoughts and feelings to understand them more clearly. And if you struggle with stress, depression, or anxiety, keeping a journal can help you gain control of your emotions and improve your mental health.

Keeping a journal helps you establish order when your world feels like it's in chaos. It helps you get to know yourself by revealing your innermost fears, thoughts, and feelings. Look at your writing time as personal relaxation time, a time when you de-stress and wind down. Write in a place that's relaxing and soothing—maybe with a lit candle and a cup of tea. Look forward to your journaling time, and know that you're doing something good for your mind and body.

Try these tips to help you get started with journaling:

- **Try to write every day.** To encourage yourself to write in your journal regularly, set aside a few minutes every day.
- **Make it easy.** Keep a pen and paper handy at all times so that when you want to jot down your thoughts, you can. You can also keep a journal in a computer file.
- **Write whatever feels right.** Your journal doesn't need to follow any particular structure. It's your own private arena to discuss whatever you want. Let the words flow freely without worrying about spelling mistakes or what other people might think.
- **Use your journal as you see fit.** You don't have to share your journal with anyone. If you do want to share some of your thoughts with trusted friends and loved ones but don't want to talk about them out loud, you could show them parts of your journal."

The following pages were designed to get you started. You may be a seasoned "journaler" or, perhaps, it's all new to you. Wherever you find yourself on the writing spectrum doesn't matter. My hope is that you'll engage in the process of journaling as an experiment and see what blessings you discover along the way.

Today I am feeling … _____

_____
_____
_____
_____
_____
_____
_____
_____
_____
_____
_____
_____
_____
_____
_____
_____
_____
_____
_____
_____
_____
_____
_____
_____
_____
_____
_____
_____
_____
_____
_____
_____
_____
_____
_____
_____

"Grief at first is natural when we think we've lost someone we love, but love never dies, it just changes form and soars on new wings up above."
Author Unknown

Today I accept … _____

_____

_____

_____

_____

_____

_____

_____

_____

_____

_____

_____

_____

_____

_____

_____

_____

_____

_____

_____

_____

_____

_____

_____

_____

_____

_____

_____

_____

_____

_____

_____

_____

_____

_____

"There's so much grace in acceptance. It's not an easy concept, but if you embrace it, you'll find more peace than you ever imagined."
Loretta LaRoche

Today I am noticing … _____

_____

_____

_____

_____

_____

_____

_____

_____

_____

_____

_____

_____

_____

_____

_____

_____

_____

_____

_____

_____

_____

_____

_____

_____

_____

_____

_____

_____

_____

_____

_____

_____

_____

"Be mindful of your self-talk. It's a conversation with the universe."
David James Lee

Today I surrender... _____

_____

_____

_____

_____

_____

_____

_____

_____

_____

_____

_____

_____

_____

_____

_____

_____

_____

_____

_____

_____

_____

_____

_____

_____

_____

_____

_____

_____

_____

_____

_____

_____

_____

_____

_____

_____

"Bring acceptance into your non-acceptance. Bring surrender into your non-surrender.
Then see what happens."
Eckhart Tolle

Today I choose to ... _____

_____

_____

_____

_____

_____

_____

_____

_____

_____

_____

_____

_____

_____

_____

_____

_____

_____

_____

_____

_____

_____

_____

_____

_____

_____

_____

_____

_____

_____

_____

_____

_____

_____

"The only way to discover the limits of the possible is to go beyond them into the impossible."
Arthur C. Clarke

Today I am grateful for ... _____

_____

_____

_____

_____

_____

_____

_____

_____

_____

_____

_____

_____

_____

_____

_____

_____

_____

_____

_____

_____

_____

_____

_____

_____

_____

_____

_____

_____

_____

_____

_____

_____

_____

_____

"Don't cry because it's over. Smile because it happened."
Dr. Seuss

Today I am feeling ... _____

_____

_____

_____

_____

_____

_____

_____

_____

_____

_____

_____

_____

_____

_____

_____

_____

_____

_____

_____

_____

_____

_____

_____

_____

_____

_____

_____

_____

_____

_____

_____

_____

"The best and most beautiful things in the world cannot be seen or even touched—they must be felt with the heart."
Helen Keller

Today I accept ... _____

_____
_____
_____
_____
_____
_____
_____
_____
_____
_____
_____
_____
_____
_____
_____
_____
_____
_____
_____
_____
_____
_____
_____
_____
_____
_____
_____
_____
_____
_____
_____
_____
_____
_____
_____
_____
_____

"There are moments which mark your life. Moments when you realize nothing will ever be the same and time is divided into two parts, before this and after this."
John Hobbes

Today I am noticing … _____

_____

_____

_____

_____

_____

_____

_____

_____

_____

_____

_____

_____

_____

_____

_____

_____

_____

_____

_____

_____

_____

_____

_____

_____

_____

_____

_____

_____

_____

_____

_____

_____

_____

_____

_____

"Mindfulness means paying attention in a particular way, on purpose, in the present moment non-judgmentally."
Jon Kabat Zinn

Today I surrender... _____

_____
_____
_____
_____
_____
_____
_____
_____
_____
_____
_____
_____
_____
_____
_____
_____
_____
_____
_____
_____
_____
_____
_____
_____
_____
_____
_____
_____
_____
_____
_____
_____
_____
_____
_____
_____
_____
_____

"If you surrender completely to the moments as they pass, you live more richly those moments."
Anne Morrow Lindbergh

Today I choose to ... _____

_____

_____

_____

_____

_____

_____

_____

_____

_____

_____

_____

_____

_____

_____

_____

_____

_____

_____

_____

_____

_____

_____

_____

_____

_____

_____

_____

_____

_____

_____

_____

_____

_____

_____

"You give birth to that on which you fix your mind."
Antoine de Saint-Exupery

Today I am grateful for ... _____

_____

_____

_____

_____

_____

_____

_____

_____

_____

_____

_____

_____

_____

_____

_____

_____

_____

_____

_____

_____

_____

_____

_____

_____

_____

_____

_____

_____

_____

_____

_____

_____

_____

"Everyone has inside of him a piece of good news. The good news is that you don't know how great you can be! How much you can love! What you can accomplish! And what your potential is!"
Anne Frank

Today I am feeling ... _____

_____

_____

_____

_____

_____

_____

_____

_____

_____

_____

_____

_____

_____

_____

_____

_____

_____

_____

_____

_____

_____

_____

_____

_____

_____

_____

_____

_____

_____

_____

_____

_____

_____

"It is during our darkest moments that we must focus to see the light."
Aristotle Onassis

Today I accept ... _____

_____
_____
_____
_____
_____
_____
_____
_____
_____
_____
_____
_____
_____
_____
_____
_____
_____
_____
_____
_____
_____
_____
_____
_____
_____
_____
_____
_____
_____
_____
_____
_____
_____
_____
_____

"Accept the things to which fate binds you, and love the people with whom fate brings you together, but do so with all your heart."
Marcus Aurelius

Today I am noticing … _____

_____

_____

_____

_____

_____

_____

_____

_____

_____

_____

_____

_____

_____

_____

_____

_____

_____

_____

_____

_____

_____

_____

_____

_____

_____

_____

_____

_____

_____

_____

_____

_____

_____

_____

"The most precious gift we can offer others is our presence. When mindfulness embraces those we love, they will bloom like flowers."
Thich Nhat Hanh

Today I surrender... _____

_____

"On the still calm waters of surrender, the reflections of clarity appear."
Bryant McGill

Today I choose to … _____

_____

_____

_____

_____

_____

_____

_____

_____

_____

_____

_____

_____

_____

_____

_____

_____

_____

_____

_____

_____

_____

_____

_____

_____

_____

_____

_____

_____

_____

_____

_____

_____

_____

"Life is like a camera. Just focus on what's important and capture the good times, develop from the negatives and if things don't turn out, just take another shot."
Author Unknown

Today I am grateful for ..._____

_____

_____

_____

_____

_____

_____

_____

_____

_____

_____

_____

_____

_____

_____

_____

_____

_____

_____

_____

_____

_____

_____

_____

_____

_____

_____

_____

_____

_____

_____

_____

_____

_____

"Remember happiness doesn't depend upon who you are or what you have; it depends solely on what you think."
Buddha

Today I am feeling ... _____

_____

_____

_____

_____

_____

_____

_____

_____

_____

_____

_____

_____

_____

_____

_____

_____

_____

_____

_____

_____

_____

_____

_____

_____

_____

_____

_____

_____

_____

_____

_____

_____

"Grief is a normal and natural response to loss. It is originally an unlearned feeling process. Keeping grief inside increases your pain."
Anne Grant

Today I accept ... _____

_____
_____
_____
_____
_____
_____
_____
_____
_____
_____
_____
_____
_____
_____
_____
_____
_____
_____
_____
_____
_____
_____
_____
_____
_____
_____
_____
_____
_____
_____
_____
_____
_____
_____
_____

"Some people think that to be strong is to never feel pain. In reality, the strongest people are the ones who feel it, understand it, and accept it."
Author Unknown

Today I am noticing … _____

_____

_____

_____

_____

_____

_____

_____

_____

_____

_____

_____

_____

_____

_____

_____

_____

_____

_____

_____

_____

_____

_____

_____

_____

_____

_____

_____

_____

_____

_____

_____

_____

_____

_____

_____

"When we are mindful, deeply in touch with the present moment, our understanding of what is going on deepens, and we begin to be filled with acceptance, joy, peace, and love."
Thich Nhat Hanh

Today I surrender... _____

_____

"Surrender to what is, let go of what was, have faith in what will be."
Sonia Ricotti

Today I choose to ... _____

_____

_____

_____

"Turn your face to the sun and the shadows fall behind you."
Author Unknown

Today I am grateful for ... _____

_____
_____
_____
_____
_____
_____
_____
_____
_____
_____
_____
_____
_____
_____
_____
_____
_____
_____
_____
_____
_____
_____
_____
_____
_____
_____
_____
_____
_____
_____
_____
_____

"Once I knew only darkness and stillness... my life was without past or future... but a little word from the fingers of another fell into my hand that clutched at emptiness, and my heart leaped to the rapture of living."
Helen Keller

Today I am feeling … _____

_____

_____

_____

_____

_____

_____

_____

_____

_____

_____

_____

_____

_____

_____

_____

_____

_____

_____

_____

_____

_____

_____

_____

_____

_____

_____

_____

_____

_____

_____

_____

_____

_____

_____

_____

"When you are sorrowful look again in your heart, and you shall see that in truth you are weeping for that which has been your delight."
Kahlil Gibran

Today I accept ... _____

_____

_____

_____

_____

_____

_____

_____

_____

_____

_____

_____

_____

_____

_____

_____

_____

_____

_____

_____

_____

_____

_____

_____

_____

_____

_____

_____

_____

_____

_____

_____

_____

_____

_____

_____

_____

"My happiness grows in direct proportion to my acceptance, and in inverse proportion to my expectations."
Michael J. Fox

Today I am noticing ... _____

_____

_____

_____

_____

_____

_____

_____

_____

_____

_____

_____

_____

_____

_____

_____

_____

_____

_____

_____

_____

_____

_____

_____

_____

_____

_____

_____

_____

_____

_____

_____

_____

_____

_____

"Realize deeply that the present moment is all you ever have."
Eckhart Tolle

Today I trust … _____

_____
_____
_____
_____
_____
_____
_____
_____
_____
_____
_____
_____
_____
_____
_____
_____
_____
_____
_____
_____
_____
_____
_____
_____
_____
_____
_____
_____
_____
_____
_____
_____
_____
_____

"To love means loving the unlovable. To forgive means pardoning the unpardonable. Faith means believing the unbelievable. Hope means hoping when everything seems hopeless."
Gilbert K. Chesterton

Today I choose to ... _____

_____

_____

_____

_____

_____

_____

_____

_____

_____

_____

_____

_____

_____

_____

_____

_____

_____

_____

_____

_____

_____

_____

_____

_____

_____

_____

_____

_____

_____

_____

_____

_____

"The brain simply believes what you tell it most. And what you tell it about you, it will create. It has no choice."
Chandler Fuller

Today I am grateful for ... _____

_____

_____

_____

_____

_____

_____

_____

_____

_____

_____

_____

_____

_____

_____

_____

_____

_____

_____

_____

_____

_____

_____

_____

_____

_____

_____

_____

_____

_____

_____

_____

_____

_____

_____

"Happiness cannot be traveled to, owned, earned, worn or consumed. Happiness is the spiritual experience of living every minute with love, grace, and gratitude."
Denis Waitley

Today I am feeling ..._____

_____

_____

_____

_____

_____

_____

_____

_____

_____

_____

_____

_____

_____

_____

_____

_____

_____

_____

_____

_____

_____

_____

_____

_____

_____

_____

_____

_____

_____

_____

_____

_____

_____

_____

_____

"Grief isn't something you get over, it's something you go through."
Alan Pedersen

Today I accept … _____

_____

_____

_____

_____

_____

_____

_____

_____

_____

_____

_____

_____

_____

_____

_____

_____

_____

_____

_____

_____

_____

_____

_____

_____

_____

_____

_____

_____

_____

_____

_____

_____

_____

_____

_____

"Whatever you accept completely will take you to peace, including the acceptance that you cannot accept, that you are in resistance."
Eckhart Tolle

Today I am noticing ... _____

_____
_____
_____
_____
_____
_____
_____
_____
_____
_____
_____
_____
_____
_____
_____
_____
_____
_____
_____
_____
_____
_____
_____
_____
_____
_____
_____
_____
_____
_____
_____
_____
_____
_____
_____

"There has to be an intention to pay attention in the present moment because it's the only moment."
Jon Kabat Zinn

Today I trust … _____

_____

_____

_____

_____

_____

_____

_____

_____

_____

_____

_____

_____

_____

_____

_____

_____

_____

_____

_____

_____

_____

_____

_____

_____

_____

_____

_____

_____

_____

_____

_____

_____

_____

"Give light, and the darkness will disappear of itself."
Desiderius Erasmus

Today I choose to ... _____

_____

_____

_____

_____

_____

_____

_____

_____

_____

_____

_____

_____

_____

_____

_____

_____

_____

_____

_____

_____

_____

_____

_____

_____

_____

_____

_____

_____

_____

_____

_____

_____

_____

_____

_____

_____

_____

_____

"Start by doing what's necessary; then do what's possible; and suddenly you are doing the impossible."
St. Francis of Assisi

Today I am grateful for ... _____

_____

_____

_____

_____

_____

_____

_____

_____

_____

_____

_____

_____

_____

_____

_____

_____

_____

_____

_____

_____

_____

_____

_____

_____

_____

_____

_____

_____

_____

_____

_____

_____

_____

_____

_____

"Happiness resides not in possessions, and not in gold, happiness dwells in the soul."
Democritus

Today I am feeling … _____

_____

_____

_____

_____

_____

_____

_____

_____

_____

_____

_____

_____

_____

_____

_____

_____

_____

_____

_____

_____

_____

_____

_____

_____

_____

_____

_____

_____

_____

_____

_____

_____

_____

_____

"The only people who think there's a time limit for grief, have never lost a piece of their heart. Take all the time you need."
Author Unknown

Today I accept ... _____

_____
_____
_____
_____
_____
_____
_____
_____
_____
_____
_____
_____
_____
_____
_____
_____
_____
_____
_____
_____
_____
_____
_____
_____
_____
_____
_____
_____
_____
_____
_____
_____
_____
_____
_____

"Acceptance doesn't mean resignation. It means understanding that something is what it is and there's got to be a way through it."
Michael J. Fox

Today I am noticing ... _____

_____

_____

_____

_____

_____

_____

_____

_____

_____

_____

_____

_____

_____

_____

_____

_____

_____

_____

_____

_____

_____

_____

_____

_____

_____

_____

_____

_____

_____

_____

_____

_____

"To the mind that is still, the whole universe surrenders."
Lao Tzu

Today I trust … _____

_____
_____
_____
_____
_____
_____
_____
_____
_____
_____
_____
_____
_____
_____
_____
_____
_____
_____
_____
_____
_____
_____
_____
_____
_____
_____
_____
_____
_____
_____
_____
_____
_____
_____

"There is nothing in a caterpillar that tells you it's going to be a butterfly."
Buckminster Fuller

Today I choose to ... _____

_____

_____

_____

_____

_____

_____

_____

_____

_____

_____

_____

_____

_____

_____

_____

_____

_____

_____

_____

_____

_____

_____

_____

_____

_____

_____

_____

_____

_____

_____

_____

_____

_____

_____

"Don't wait for inspiration. Take action. Action generates inspiration."
Frank Tibolt

Today I am grateful for ... _____

_____

_____

_____

_____

_____

_____

_____

_____

_____

_____

_____

_____

_____

_____

_____

_____

_____

_____

_____

_____

_____

_____

_____

_____

_____

_____

_____

_____

_____

_____

_____

_____

_____

_____

_____

_____

"I have always believed, and I still believe, that whatever good or bad fortune may come our way we can always give it meaning and transform it into something of value."
Hermann Hesse

Today I am feeling ... _____

_____
_____
_____
_____
_____
_____
_____
_____
_____
_____
_____
_____
_____
_____
_____
_____
_____
_____
_____
_____
_____
_____
_____
_____
_____
_____
_____
_____
_____
_____
_____
_____
_____
_____
_____
_____
_____

"Grief is like a long valley, a winding valley where any bend may reveal a totally new landscape."
C. S. Lewis

Today I am noticing … _____

_____
_____
_____
_____
_____
_____
_____
_____
_____
_____
_____
_____
_____
_____
_____
_____
_____
_____
_____
_____
_____
_____
_____
_____
_____
_____
_____
_____
_____
_____
_____
_____
_____

"I did not come to my fundamental understanding of the universe through my rational mind."
Albert Einstein

Today I forgive … _____

_____
_____
_____
_____
_____
_____
_____
_____
_____
_____
_____
_____
_____
_____
_____
_____
_____
_____
_____
_____
_____
_____
_____
_____
_____
_____
_____
_____
_____
_____
_____
_____
_____
_____
_____

"To forgive is to set a prisoner free, and realize the prisoner was you."
Author Unknown

Today I send a blessing to ... _____

_____
_____
_____
_____
_____
_____
_____
_____
_____
_____
_____
_____
_____
_____
_____
_____
_____
_____
_____
_____
_____
_____
_____
_____
_____
_____
_____
_____
_____
_____
_____
_____
_____
_____
_____
_____
_____
_____

"Learning how to be still, to really be still and let life happen - that stillness becomes a radiance."
Morgan Freeman

Today I choose to ... _____

_____

_____

_____

_____

_____

_____

_____

_____

_____

_____

_____

_____

_____

_____

_____

_____

_____

_____

_____

_____

_____

_____

_____

_____

_____

_____

_____

_____

_____

_____

_____

"I can't change the direction of the wind, but I can adjust my sails to always reach my destination."
Jimmy Dean

Today I am grateful for ... _____

_____

_____

_____

_____

_____

_____

_____

_____

_____

_____

_____

_____

_____

_____

_____

_____

_____

_____

_____

_____

_____

_____

_____

_____

_____

_____

_____

_____

"We all have the extraordinary coded within us waiting to be released."
Jean Houston

Today I am feeling … _____

_____

_____

_____

_____

_____

_____

_____

_____

_____

_____

_____

_____

_____

_____

_____

_____

_____

_____

_____

_____

_____

_____

_____

_____

_____

_____

_____

_____

_____

_____

_____

_____

"Feeling sorry for yourself, and your present condition, is not only a waste of energy but the worst habit you could possibly have."
Dale Carnegie

Today I am noticing … _____

_____

_____

_____

_____

_____

_____

_____

_____

_____

_____

_____

_____

_____

_____

_____

_____

_____

_____

_____

_____

_____

_____

_____

_____

_____

_____

_____

_____

_____

_____

_____

_____

_____

_____

"Worry doesn't prevent tomorrow's sorrows. But it will steal today's joy."
Clare Josa

Today I forgive … _____

_____

_____

_____

_____

_____

_____

_____

_____

_____

_____

_____

_____

_____

_____

_____

_____

_____

_____

_____

_____

_____

_____

_____

_____

_____

_____

_____

_____

_____

_____

_____

"If we really want to love, we must learn how to forgive."
Mother Theresa

Today I send a blessing to ... _____

_____

_____

_____

_____

_____

_____

_____

_____

_____

_____

_____

_____

_____

_____

_____

_____

_____

_____

_____

_____

_____

_____

_____

_____

_____

_____

_____

_____

_____

_____

_____

_____

_____

_____

"If you could only love enough, you could be the most powerful person in the world."
Emmet Fox

Today I choose to ... _____

_____

_____

_____

_____

_____

_____

_____

_____

_____

_____

_____

_____

_____

_____

_____

_____

_____

_____

_____

_____

_____

_____

_____

_____

_____

_____

_____

_____

_____

_____

_____

_____

_____

_____

"The most authentic thing about us is our capacity to create, to overcome, to endure, to transform, to love and to be greater than our suffering."
Ben Okri

Today I am grateful for ... _____

_____

_____

_____

_____

_____

_____

_____

_____

_____

_____

_____

_____

_____

_____

_____

_____

_____

_____

_____

_____

_____

_____

_____

_____

_____

_____

_____

_____

_____

_____

_____

_____

"As we express our gratitude, we must never forget that the highest appreciation is not to utter words, but to live by them."
President John F. Kennedy

Today I am feeling … _____

_____

_____

_____

_____

_____

_____

_____

_____

_____

_____

_____

_____

_____

_____

_____

_____

_____

_____

_____

_____

_____

_____

_____

_____

_____

_____

_____

_____

_____

_____

_____

_____

_____

_____

_____

"All the elements for your happiness are already here. There is no need to run, strive, search, or struggle. Just be."
Thich Nhat Hanh

Today I am noticing ... _____

_____

_____

_____

_____

_____

_____

_____

_____

_____

_____

_____

_____

_____

_____

_____

_____

_____

_____

_____

_____

_____

_____

_____

_____

_____

_____

_____

_____

_____

_____

_____

_____

"Look within. Within is the fountain of good, and it will ever bubble up, if thou wilt ever dig."
Marcus Aurelius

Today I forgive … _____

_____

_____

_____

"Forgiveness does not change the past, but it does enlarge the future."
Paul Boese

Today I send a blessing to ... _____

_____
_____
_____
_____
_____
_____
_____
_____
_____
_____
_____
_____
_____
_____
_____
_____
_____
_____
_____
_____
_____
_____
_____
_____
_____
_____
_____
_____
_____
_____
_____
_____

"Try to be a rainbow in someone's cloud."
Maya Angelou

Today I choose to … _____

_____

_____

_____

_____

_____

_____

_____

_____

_____

_____

_____

_____

_____

_____

_____

_____

_____

_____

_____

_____

_____

_____

_____

_____

_____

_____

_____

_____

_____

_____

_____

_____

_____

"At least once a day, allow yourself to think and dream for yourself."
Albert Einstein

Today I am grateful for … _____

_____
_____
_____
_____
_____
_____
_____
_____
_____
_____
_____
_____
_____
_____
_____
_____
_____
_____
_____
_____
_____
_____
_____
_____
_____
_____
_____
_____
_____
_____
_____
_____
_____
_____
_____

"The fact that I can plant a seed and it becomes a flower, share a bit of knowledge and it becomes another's, smile at someone and receive a smile in return, are to me continual spiritual exercises."
Leo Buscaglia

Today I am feeling ... _____

_____
_____
_____
_____
_____
_____
_____
_____
_____
_____
_____
_____
_____
_____
_____
_____
_____
_____
_____
_____
_____
_____
_____
_____
_____
_____
_____
_____
_____
_____
_____
_____
_____
_____
_____
_____
_____

"Sometimes your joy is the source of your smile, but sometimes your smile can be the source of your joy."
Thich Nhat Hanh

Today I am noticing ... _____

_____

_____

_____

_____

_____

_____

_____

_____

_____

_____

_____

_____

_____

_____

_____

_____

_____

_____

_____

_____

_____

_____

_____

_____

_____

_____

_____

_____

_____

_____

_____

"Miracles are a retelling in small letters of the very same story which is written across the whole world in letters too large for some of us to see."
C. S. Lewis

Today I forgive … _____

_____
_____
_____
_____
_____
_____
_____
_____
_____
_____
_____
_____
_____
_____
_____
_____
_____
_____
_____
_____
_____
_____
_____
_____
_____
_____
_____
_____
_____
_____
_____
_____
_____
_____
_____

"He who is devoid of the power to forgive is devoid of the power to love. There is some good in the worst of us and some evil in the best of us. When we discover this, we are less prone to hate our enemies."
Martin Luther King, Jr.

Today I send a blessing to ... _____

_____
_____
_____
_____
_____
_____
_____
_____
_____
_____
_____
_____
_____
_____
_____
_____
_____
_____
_____
_____
_____
_____
_____
_____
_____
_____
_____
_____
_____
_____
_____
_____
_____

"From what we get, we can make a living; what we give, however, makes a life."
Arthur Ashe

Today I choose to ... _____

_____

_____

_____

_____

_____

_____

_____

_____

_____

_____

_____

_____

_____

_____

_____

_____

_____

_____

_____

_____

_____

_____

_____

_____

_____

_____

_____

_____

_____

_____

_____

_____

_____

"When you get into a tight place and everything goes against you, till it seems as though you could not hang on a minute longer, never give up then, for that is just the place and time that the tide will turn."
Harriet Beecher Stowe

Today I am grateful for ... _____

_____

_____

_____

_____

_____

_____

_____

_____

_____

_____

_____

_____

_____

_____

_____

_____

_____

_____

_____

_____

_____

_____

_____

_____

_____

_____

_____

_____

_____

_____

_____

_____

"Gratitude is an opener of locked-up blessings."
Marianne Williamson

Today I am feeling … _____

_____

_____

_____

_____

_____

_____

_____

_____

_____

_____

_____

_____

_____

_____

_____

_____

_____

_____

_____

_____

_____

_____

_____

_____

_____

_____

_____

_____

_____

_____

_____

_____

_____

_____

_____

_____

"People have a hard time letting go of their suffering. Out of a fear of the unknown, they prefer suffering that is familiar."
Thich Nhat Hanh

Today I am noticing … _____

_____

_____

_____

_____

_____

_____

_____

_____

_____

_____

_____

_____

_____

_____

_____

_____

_____

_____

_____

_____

_____

_____

_____

_____

_____

_____

_____

_____

_____

_____

_____

_____

_____

"The day you decide that you are more interested in being aware of your thoughts than you are in the thoughts themselves—that is the day you will find your way out."
Michael Singer

Today I forgive ... _____

_____

_____

_____

_____

_____

_____

_____

_____

_____

_____

_____

_____

_____

_____

_____

_____

_____

_____

_____

_____

_____

_____

_____

_____

_____

_____

_____

_____

_____

_____

_____

_____

_____

_____

"If you want to see brave, look at those who can forgive."
Bahagavad Gita

Today I send a blessing to ... _____

_____

_____

_____

_____

_____

_____

_____

_____

_____

_____

_____

_____

_____

_____

_____

_____

_____

_____

_____

_____

_____

_____

_____

_____

_____

_____

_____

_____

_____

_____

_____

_____

"Death is not the greatest loss in life. The greatest loss is what dies inside us while we live."

Norman Cousins

Today I choose to … _____

_____

_____

_____

_____

_____

_____

_____

_____

_____

_____

_____

_____

_____

_____

_____

_____

_____

_____

_____

_____

_____

_____

_____

_____

_____

_____

_____

_____

_____

_____

_____

_____

_____

_____

_____

_____

"You change your life by changing your heart."
Max Lucado

Today I am grateful for … _____

_____
_____
_____
_____
_____
_____
_____
_____
_____
_____
_____
_____
_____
_____
_____
_____
_____
_____
_____
_____
_____
_____
_____
_____
_____
_____
_____
_____
_____
_____
_____
_____
_____
_____

"Like a bird singing in the rain, let grateful memories survive in time of sorrow."
Robert Louis Stevenson

Today I am feeling … _____

_____

_____

_____

_____

_____

_____

_____

_____

_____

_____

_____

_____

_____

_____

_____

_____

_____

_____

_____

_____

_____

_____

_____

_____

_____

_____

_____

_____

_____

_____

_____

_____

_____

"Happiness is a butterfly, which when pursued, is always just beyond your grasp, but which, if you will sit down quietly, may alight upon you."
Nathaniel Hawthorne

Today I am noticing … _____

_____
_____
_____
_____
_____
_____
_____
_____
_____
_____
_____
_____
_____
_____
_____
_____
_____
_____
_____
_____
_____
_____
_____
_____
_____
_____
_____
_____
_____
_____
_____
_____
_____

"The present moment is filled with joy and happiness. If you are attentive, you will see it."
Thich Nhat Hanh

Today I forgive ... _____

_____
_____
_____
_____
_____
_____
_____
_____
_____
_____
_____
_____
_____
_____
_____
_____
_____
_____
_____
_____
_____
_____
_____
_____
_____
_____
_____
_____
_____
_____
_____
_____
_____
_____
_____
_____
_____

"Bring into your mind anyone against whom you have a grievance and let it go. Send that person your forgiveness."
Deepak Chopra

Today I send a blessing to ... _____

_____

_____

_____

_____

_____

_____

_____

_____

_____

_____

_____

_____

_____

_____

_____

_____

_____

_____

_____

_____

_____

_____

_____

_____

_____

_____

_____

_____

_____

_____

_____

_____

_____

"Do your little bit of good where you are; it's those little bits of good put together that overwhelm the world."

Desmond Tutu

Today I choose to ... _____

_____

_____

_____

_____

_____

_____

_____

_____

_____

_____

_____

_____

_____

_____

_____

_____

_____

_____

_____

_____

_____

_____

_____

_____

_____

_____

_____

_____

_____

_____

_____

_____

_____

_____

_____

"I am the master of my fate; I am the captain of my soul."
William Ernest Henley

Today I am grateful for … _____

_____

_____

_____

_____

_____

_____

_____

_____

_____

_____

_____

_____

_____

_____

_____

_____

_____

_____

_____

_____

_____

_____

_____

_____

_____

_____

_____

_____

_____

_____

_____

_____

_____

"Let your smile change the world, but don't let the world change your smile."
Author Unknown

Today I am feeling ... _____

_____

_____

_____

_____

_____

_____

_____

_____

_____

_____

_____

_____

_____

_____

_____

_____

_____

_____

_____

_____

_____

_____

_____

_____

_____

_____

_____

_____

_____

_____

_____

_____

_____

_____

_____

"The soul always knows what to do to heal itself. The challenge is to silence the mind."
Carolyn Myss

Today I am noticing ... _____

_____
_____
_____
_____
_____
_____
_____
_____
_____
_____
_____
_____
_____
_____
_____
_____
_____
_____
_____
_____
_____
_____
_____
_____
_____
_____
_____
_____
_____
_____
_____
_____
_____
_____
_____

"If you change the way you look at things, the things you look at change."
Wayne Dyer

Today I forgive ... _____

_____

_____

_____

_____

_____

_____

_____

_____

_____

_____

_____

_____

_____

_____

_____

_____

_____

_____

_____

_____

_____

_____

_____

_____

_____

_____

_____

_____

_____

_____

_____

_____

_____

_____

_____

_____

"Holding onto anger is like drinking poison and expecting the other person to die."
Buddha

Today I send a blessing to ... _____

_____

_____

_____

_____

_____

_____

_____

_____

_____

_____

_____

_____

_____

_____

_____

_____

_____

_____

_____

_____

_____

_____

_____

_____

_____

_____

_____

_____

_____

_____

_____

_____

_____

_____

"The purpose of life is to discover your gift. The meaning of life is giving your gift away."
David Viscott

Today I choose to … _____

_____
_____
_____
_____
_____
_____
_____
_____
_____
_____
_____
_____
_____
_____
_____
_____
_____
_____
_____
_____
_____
_____
_____
_____
_____
_____
_____
_____
_____
_____
_____
_____
_____
_____
_____

"I am not interested so much in what I do with my hands or words as what I do with my heart. I want to live from the inside out, not from the outside in."
Hugh Prather

Today I am grateful for ... _____

_____

_____

_____

_____

_____

_____

_____

_____

_____

_____

_____

_____

_____

_____

_____

_____

_____

_____

_____

_____

_____

_____

_____

_____

_____

_____

_____

_____

_____

_____

_____

"Happiness doesn't depend on any external conditions. It is governed by our mental attitude."
Dale Carnegie

Today I am feeling … _____

_____

_____

_____

_____

_____

_____

_____

_____

_____

_____

_____

_____

_____

_____

_____

_____

_____

_____

_____

_____

_____

_____

_____

_____

_____

_____

_____

_____

_____

_____

_____

_____

_____

_____

_____

"I will love the light for it shows me the way, yet I will endure the darkness because it shows me the stars."
Og Mandino

Today I am noticing ... _____

_____

_____

_____

_____

_____

_____

_____

_____

_____

_____

_____

_____

_____

_____

_____

_____

_____

_____

_____

_____

_____

_____

_____

_____

_____

_____

_____

_____

_____

_____

"Can you hear it? Your right brain speaks to you—and guides you—in the subtle language of impulses, feelings, hunches and intuitions. 'I get my ideas,' said Edison, 'by listening from within.'"
Zane Vaughn

Today I trust ... _____

_____

_____

_____

_____

_____

_____

_____

_____

_____

_____

_____

_____

_____

_____

_____

_____

_____

_____

_____

_____

_____

_____

_____

_____

_____

_____

_____

_____

_____

_____

_____

_____

_____

"The Wright brothers flew right through the smoke screen of impossibility."
Charles Kettering

Today I send a blessing to ... _____

_____

_____

_____

_____

_____

_____

_____

_____

_____

_____

_____

_____

_____

_____

_____

_____

_____

_____

_____

_____

_____

_____

_____

_____

_____

_____

_____

_____

_____

_____

_____

_____

_____

"Whoever is happy will make others happy too."
Anne Frank

Today I am grateful for ... _____

_____

_____

_____

_____

_____

_____

_____

_____

_____

_____

_____

_____

_____

_____

_____

_____

_____

_____

_____

_____

_____

_____

_____

_____

_____

_____

_____

_____

_____

_____

_____

"No pessimist ever discovered the secrets of the stars, or sailed to an uncharted land, or opened a new heaven to the human spirit."
Helen Keller

Today I choose to … _____

_____

_____

_____

_____

_____

_____

_____

_____

_____

_____

_____

_____

_____

_____

_____

_____

_____

_____

_____

_____

_____

_____

_____

_____

_____

_____

_____

_____

_____

_____

_____

_____

"You are today where your thoughts have brought you; you will be tomorrow where your thoughts take you."
James Allen

Today I am feeling … _____

_____
_____
_____
_____
_____
_____
_____
_____
_____
_____
_____
_____
_____
_____
_____
_____
_____
_____
_____
_____
_____
_____
_____
_____
_____
_____
_____
_____
_____
_____
_____
_____

"You can't stop the waves, but you can learn to surf."
Joseph Goldstein.

Today I am noticing … _____

_____

_____

_____

_____

_____

_____

_____

_____

_____

_____

_____

_____

_____

_____

_____

_____

_____

_____

_____

_____

_____

_____

_____

_____

_____

_____

_____

_____

_____

_____

_____

"You don't look out there for God, something in the sky, you look in you."
Alan Watts

Today I trust ... _____

_____
_____
_____
_____
_____
_____
_____
_____
_____
_____
_____
_____
_____
_____
_____
_____
_____
_____
_____
_____
_____
_____
_____
_____
_____
_____
_____
_____
_____
_____
_____
_____
_____
_____

"Man never made any material as resilient as the human spirit."
Bernard Williams

Today I send a blessing to ... _____

_____

_____

_____

_____

_____

_____

_____

_____

_____

_____

_____

_____

_____

_____

_____

_____

_____

_____

_____

_____

_____

_____

_____

_____

_____

_____

_____

_____

_____

_____

_____

"Thousands of candles can be lighted from a single candle, and the life of the candle will not be shortened. Happiness never decreases by being shared."
Buddha

Today I am grateful for … _____

_____

_____

_____

_____

_____

_____

_____

_____

_____

_____

_____

_____

_____

_____

_____

_____

_____

_____

_____

_____

_____

_____

_____

_____

_____

_____

_____

_____

_____

_____

_____

_____

_____

_____

_____

"At times, our own light goes out and is rekindled by a spark from another person. Each of us has cause to think with deep gratitude of those who have lighted the flame within us."
Albert Schweitzer

Today I choose to ... _____

_____

_____

_____

_____

_____

_____

_____

_____

_____

_____

_____

_____

_____

_____

_____

_____

_____

_____

_____

_____

_____

_____

_____

_____

_____

_____

_____

_____

_____

_____

_____

_____

_____

_____

"Happiness resides not in possessions and not in gold, happiness dwells in the soul."
Democritis

Today I am noticing ... _____

_____

_____

_____

_____

_____

_____

_____

_____

_____

_____

_____

_____

_____

_____

_____

_____

_____

_____

_____

_____

_____

_____

_____

_____

_____

_____

_____

_____

_____

_____

_____

_____

_____

_____

_____

"Realize deeply that the present moment is all you ever have."
Eckhart Tolle

About the Author

Robyn DeLong is a successful top-producing Realtor in Sacramento, CA. When moving matters, she delights in helping people dream up what's next. She is a former college professor with a Masters in Interpersonal Communication, a published poet, and a speaker and author on the topic of exploring grief as a doorway into personal growth and transformation. She has appeared on the Sacramento cable network and has been trained as a transformational life coach by some of the best, including Mary Morrissey, Bob Proctor, Jack Canfield, and Maria Nemeth. Robyn loves teaching people how to achieve new heights of success, meaning, and spiritual aliveness.

Robyn lives in Sacramento with her mini-Schnauzer Chewie. Her oldest son, Troy Ortego, is a builder and remodeling contractor working in Stanley, Idaho. He has a son named Riley. Middle son, John Ortego, is a pharmacist and owns Parkside Pharmacy and Wellness Center in Sacramento with his wife Michelle. They have three sons—oldest being Isaiah followed by identical twins, Josiah and Judah. Robyn's mom, Barbara Spengler, lives nearby, and every Sunday they can be found seated together at their local Unity Church, Spiritual Life Center. Robyn teaches personal transformation courses at her church and to her fellow Realtors at Coldwell Banker. She loves volunteering as a member of the Rotary Club of Sacramento where she has served since 2001.

Robyn says about herself, "I coach people in possibility thinking. I love helping people dream up what's next. The sudden accidental death of my youngest son, Michael Ortego, in 2013, plunged me into the depths of grief and taught me that even in unspeakable sorrow I could find hope and healing. Since Michael's death, I have been passionate about how we can use the power of grief to open doorways into new, more powerful ways of saying "yes" to life. I believe our grief can be the ground from which we grow our heart and nurture our soul.

"Like many others I've met, I had always wanted to write a book. I would come up with titles and ideas, mostly non-fiction, but the actual books only existed on that famous "Someday I'll." I wrote poetry for myself and friends, articles for newsletters, edited countless brochures and promotional pieces, and even got paid for a couple of the articles. Books and blogs authored by me only lived in my imagination. Until tragedy struck. I've learned that sometimes getting shocked into action is exactly what it takes.

"My personal journey from grief to grace has become one of my greatest lessons for finding the good in whatever comes my way. It unleashed my writing. I captured the full story of my son Resh Michael and myself in *From Grief to Grace...A Mother's Journey*, a book that would not let me alone until I completed it. I also published the book *Moments of Stillness,* a collection of inspirational poems that had been sitting dormant in my computer for almost 10 years.

"My hope is that the process of journaling for readers that can begin with this book will continue well beyond these pages and fill many personal journals, bringing the healing and the peace that I discovered when I stepped into the upward healing spiral."

Robyn is available for speaking, coaching, and weekend healing retreats. She can be reached by email: info@grieftograce.com. More about her son and their journey can be found at www.grieftograce.com. The beginnings of her blog are at www.listentoyourangels.com Robyn is also on Facebook and LinkedIn. Always ready to help people buy or sell residential real estate, her Coldwell Banker website is: www.DeLongTeam.com.

Appendix

<u>Books I read in the first 18 months following Michael's death</u>. . .

Anderson, George, Barone, Andrew: *Ask George Anderson: What Souls in the Hereafter Can Teach Us About Life*

Anthony, Mark: *Evidence of Eternity: Communicating with Spirits for Proof of the Afterlife*

Arcangel, Dianne: *Afterlife Encounters: Ordinary People, Extraordinary Experiences*

Assante PhD, Julia: *The Last Frontier: Exploring the Afterlife and Transforming Our Fear of Death*

Bertoldi, Concetta: *Inside the Other Side: Soul Contracts, Life Lessons, and How Dead People Help Us, Between Here and Heaven*

Borgia, Anthony: *Life in the World Unseen*

Botkin, Allan, Hogan, R. Craig: *Induced After-Death Communication: A New Therapy for Healing Grief and Trauma*

Burpo, Todd, Sonja Burpo, Colton Burpo: *Heaven is for Real: A Little Boy's Astounding Story of His Trip to Heaven and Back*

Carter, Chris: *Science and the Afterlife Experience: Evidence for the Immortality of Consciousness*

Champlain, Sandra: *We Don't Die: A Skeptic's Discovery of Life After Death*

Dalzell, George E.: *Messages: Evidence for Life After Death*

Daniel, Terri: *A Swan in Heaven: Conversations Between Two Worlds*

Daniel, Terri: *Turning the Corner on Grief Street: Loss and Bereavement as a Journey of Awakening*

Dispenza Dr., Joe: *You Are the Placebo: Making Your Mind Matter*

Dispenza Dr., Joe: *Evolve Your Brain: The Science of Changing Your Mind*

DuBois, Allison: *Secrets of the Monarch: What the Dead Can Teach Us About Living a Better Life*

DuBois, Allison: *Talk to Me*

DuBois, Allison: *Don't Kiss Them Good-bye*

Eldon, Kathy: *Angel Catcher: A Journal of Loss and Remembrance*

Farrimond, Erica: *Soothe your soul from grief - A mother's inspiration after losing her two year old daughter to cancer*

Frederick, Sue: *Bridges to Heaven: True Stories of Loved Ones on the Other Side*

Guggenheim, Bill, Guggenheim, Judy: *Hello from Heaven: A New Field of Research-After-Death Communication Confirms That Life and Love Are Eternal*

Hogan, R. Craig, Wright, Rochelle: *Guided Afterlife Connections*

Hummel, Virginia Michelle: *Miracle Messenger: Signs from Above, Love from Beyond*

James, John W: *The Grief Recovery Handbook, 20th Anniversary Expanded Edition: The Action Program for Moving Beyond Death, Divorce, and Other Losses including Health*

Kagan, Annie: *The Afterlife of Billy Fingers: How My Bad-Boy Brother Proved to Me There's Life After Death*

Keresey, Priscilla: *It Will All Make Sense When You're Dead: Messages From Our Loved Ones in the Spirit World*

Klein, Kimberly: *The Universe Speaks: A Heavenly Dialogue*

Klein, Kimberly: *Hummingbirds Don't Fly In The Rain: A mothers extraordinary search for her daughter in this life- and the next*

Lewis, Scarlett: *Nurturing Healing Love: A Mother's Journey of Hope and Forgiveness*

Martin, Michael: *When Spirit Speaks*

Mathews, Patrick: *Forever With You: Inspiring Messages of Healing & Wisdom from your Loved Ones in the Afterlife*

Mathews, Patrick: *Never Say Goodbye: A Medium's Stories of Connecting With Your Loved Ones*

Medhus M.D. ,Elisa: *My Son and the Afterlife: Conversations from the Other Side*

Moody Jr.,Raymond: *Reunions: Visionary Encounters With Departed Loved Ones Mass Market Paperback*

Noé, Karen: *Through the Eyes of Another: A Medium's Guide to Creating Heaven on Earth by Encountering Your Life Review Now*

Noé, Karen: *The Rainbow Follows the Storm: How to Obtain Inner Peace by Connecting with Angels and Deceased Loved Ones*

Noé, Karen: *Your Life After Their Death: A Medium's Guide to Healing After a Loss*

Obley, Carole J.: *I'm Still With You: True Stories of Healing Grief Through Spirit Communication.*

Occhino, MaryRose: *Beyond These Four Walls: Diary of a Psychic Medium*

Olson, Bob: *Answers about the Afterlife: A Private Investigator's 15-Year Research Unlocks the Mysteries of Life after Death*

Pascuzzi, Robert: *The Ravine*

Pepin, Eric: *Igniting the Sixth Sense: The Lost Human Sensory that Holds the Key to Spiritual Awakening and Unlocking the Power of the Universe*

Pettigrew, Mike: *Afterlife: Startling Evidence for Life After Death*

Piper, Don: Murphey, Cecil: *90 Minutes in Heaven: A True Story of Death & Life*

Radin PhD, Dean: *The Conscious Universe: The Scientific Truth of Psychic Phenomena*

Rathore, Michelle: *Spirit Nudges: Proof That Spirit Is Never Far Away*

Robinett, Kristy: *Messenger Between Worlds: True Stories from a Psychic Medium*

Scavetta, Heather: *The Power of Love: A Mother's Miraculous Journey from Grief to Medium, Channel, and Teacher*

Schwartz, Gary E.: *The Afterlife Experiments: Breakthrough Scientific Evidence of Life After Death*

Schwartz, Gary E., Simon, William L: *The Truth about Medium: Extraordinary Experiments with the Real Allison DuBois of NBC's Medium and other Remarkable Psychics*

Singer, Michael: *The Surrender Experiment: My Journey into Life's Perfection*

Sinor, Barbara: *The Pact: Messages from the Other Side*

Smith, Gordon: *Through My Eyes*

Stafford, Betty: *The Afterlife Unveiled: What the Dead are Telling Us About Their World*

Steiner, Rudolf: *Staying Connected*

Taylor, Greg: *Stop Worrying! There Probably is an Afterlife*

Terri Daniel: *Embracing Death: A New Look at Grief, Gratitude and God*

Tucci, Kathleen: *Vibrating To Spirit: A Psychic's Journey to the Other Side*

Van Praagh, James: *Unfinished Business: What the Dead Can Teach Us About Life*

Van Praagh, James: *Heaven and Earth: Making the Psychic Connection*

Van Praagh, James: *Talking to Heaven: A Medium's Message of Life After Death*

Virtue, Doreen: *Talking to Heaven Mediumship Cards: A 44-Card Deck and Guidebook*

Virtue, Doreen: *How to Heal a Grieving Heart*

Zammit, Victor, Zammit, Wendy: *A Lawyer Presents the Evidence for the Afterlife*

Zuba, Tom: *Permission to Mourn: A New Way to Do Grief*

Acknowledgments

Thank you Mary Morrissey for your teaching and coaching over the last 17 years. Many of the stories in this book were new to me until I heard Mary tell them. I always delight in Mary's stories no matter how many times I've heard them. She is a master teacher.

Thank you Stu Boyer for again creating a beautiful cover for this book as you did for *From Grief to Grace...A Mother's Journey.* Thank you for the love and friendship and all that you have done to keep Michael's music and memory alive. You and Michael were quite the team, and I know he still watches over you.

Thank you to all of today's pioneers who are studying life after death, near death experiences, and the mind-body-spirit connection. And, thank you to those who launched the transcendental movement in the late 1800s beginning with the Concord Conversations: Ralph Waldo Emerson, Henry David Thoreau, William James, Walt Whitman, the Alcotts, followed by Mary Baker Eddy, Charles and Myrtle Fillmore, and Ernest Holmes.

I'm grateful for all of the teachers and writers whose works have made an impact on my life. If I were to name them all, the contents of my library would flood these pages. Key books and authors are: *As a Man Thinketh*, by James Allen; *Your Invisible Power,* by Genevieve Behrend; *The Master Key System,* by Charles Haanel; *Think and Grow Rich,* by Napoleon Hill; *Working with the Law,* by Raymond Holliwell; *Building your Field of Dreams,* by Mary Morrissey; *The Power of the Spoken Word,* by Florence Scovel Shinn; *The Untethered Soul,* by Michael Singer; *The Wisdom of Wallace Wattles,* by Wallace D. Wattles; *The Autobiography of a Yogi,* by Paramhansa Yogananda;. I've benefited by reading entire collections from Deepak Chopra, Wayne Dyer, Eckhart Tolle, Jack Canfield, and Joe Dispenza.

I am profoundly grateful for my friends and family and the loving relationships that have held us together throughout all of the years. You know who you are, and I love and bless each and every one of you.

Made in the USA
Middletown, DE
26 June 2015